RECIPES FOR LIFE
Fifty Ready-To-Use
Spiritual Talks For Children

Vanessa Wyse Jackson is a former secondary teacher with additional experience as a National Trainer with the Irish Girl Guides. In her present capacity as the minister in Rathgar Methodist Church in Dublin she is also chaplain to Rathgar National School, where she has taken weekly assemblies since 2006. She is married to Patrick and they have two daughters, Susanna and Katie.

D0416080

RECIPES
FOR LIFE

Fifty Ready-To-Use
Spiritual Talks For
Children

Vanessa Wyse Jackson

VERITAS

Published 2012 by
Veritas Publications
7–8 Lower Abbey Street
Dublin 1, Ireland
publications@veritas.ie
www.veritas.ie

ISBN 978 1 84730 360 8
Copyright © Vanessa Wyse Jackson, 2012

10 9 8 7 6 5 4 3 2 1

'Seven Spools of Thread', p. 104, based on *Seven Spools of Thread: A Kwanzaa Story* by Angela Shelf. Illustrated by Daniel Minter. Published by Albert Whitman & Company. By permission of Albert Whitman & Company.

A catalogue record for this book is available from the British Library.

Cover designed by Barbara Croatto, Veritas
Printed in the Republic of Ireland by Gemini International, Dublin

Veritas books are printed on paper made from the wood pulp of managed forests. For every tree felled, at least one tree is planted, thereby renewing natural resources.

Acknowledgements

I am very grateful to the principal, staff and pupils of Rathgar National School and to the children of Rathgar Methodist Church for allowing me the opportunity to exercise and develop this ministry in their midst over the last few years. To my husband, Patrick, for his technical expertise and unfailing support throughout; and to our two daughters: Katie, for her feedback and encouragement, and Susanna, who provided the illustrations.

Contents

Introduction

Containing fifty tried and tested children's talks, this book is intended as a resource for teachers, clergy and youth workers as they seek to find quick, easy and creative new ideas to engage with primary school children in their care. While the talks have originated in a Christian context, many of them can also be easily adapted to work effectively in a variety of secular and multicultural settings. The book has been written with the changing face of Irish education in mind and many of the themes have been drawn from other countries and cultures in an effort to be as inclusive as possible.

PART 1
AUTUMN
HARVEST
HALLOWE'EN
THANKSGIVING

1.
Back to School

CONTEXT
An ideal talk for the first assembly of the year, especially when there are new children in the infant classes who will need something simple to focus on.

YOU WILL NEED
A well-equipped and brightly coloured pencil case containing a variety of everyday school stationery items including a pencil, eraser, ruler, colouring pencils, sharpener, ink cartridge, highlighter pen and compass.

Try to tap into the excitement of the beginning of the new school year and to share with the children something of the excitement that you may have felt as a child when you began a new school year.

Take out each item in turn and ask the children why it is important to have an item like this in school. Take the suggestions of the lower half of the school to begin with to get them engaged and involved.

Then move on to explore how we might also see our Christian lives reflected in these items. Pick up each one again to show the children. This time you may like to ask some of the older children to make suggestions as to what each item could represent in terms of their learning and development as followers of Jesus.

Some suggestions may include:
- Pencil – reminds us that God is in the ordinary things in our lives
- Ruler – keeps us on a straight path
- Eraser – gives us a fresh start when we make a mistake
- Compass – the steady centre point gives our lives the right shape
- Cartridge – a pen only does its job properly when it has the right filling
- Sharpener – reminds us of our need to keep in spiritual shape
- Colouring pencils – remind us of the variety of the world and the people around us.

CLOSING PRAYER OUTLINE
Our loving Father, we thank you for this brand new term and for all the possibilities that lie ahead. We ask that you will be with us in all our learning and discovery, guiding us and helping us day by day to become the people that you want us to be. In the name of Jesus we pray. Amen.

2.
Developing Healthy Habits

CONTEXT
Perhaps best used at the beginning of the school year or the beginning of the calendar year when the schools go back in January.

YOU WILL NEED
A ball of string, some thick wool, some thinner wool, some cotton thread (which you will be tying together in ascending order of strength) and a pair of scissors.

Talk to the children about the last week and what has been happening in their lives while you are tying the thread, wool and string together.

Emphasise the beginning of the new year and how important it is to make a good start. You might ask the children about their New Year's resolutions or any special plans they may have as they start in a new class group. Say that it is very important to get things off to a good start. Include the staff by talking about how primary school teachers are especially important because they are the people that get us all started off in life. Lead the children in a round of applause to show how much they appreciate their teachers!

Expand on this by saying that the things we do when we are very young will shape the kind of person we'll become when we're older. Reflect for a minute about the things people do. What about bad habits? Ask the assembly if anyone bites their nails, or gets their rooms into an awful mess, or fights with their brother or sister.

Tell the children that we all develop habits of one kind or another and that it's important when we start out to make sure we develop good, healthy habits. Because, as we all know, some habits can be very difficult to break.

Invite a volunteer (preferably an older child) to come up and to break the first piece of thread (which should be easy!). Talk about how some habits can become harder to break as you get older and ask the child to break the wool (also not difficult). Show how things become a little tougher as times go on (ask the child to break the thicker piece of wool (which should still be possible but with a lot more effort!) and then stop for a moment. Show the children the place where the thick wool joins on to the string and say that there is a point at which you have a last chance to change your behaviour and that this is it. After this, it will be impossible to break the habit on your own. You will need serious help from somewhere else. Cut the string with a scissors.

CLOSING PRAYER OUTLINE
Father God, we thank you for this new term/year and for the chance to make a fresh start. Help us to develop good habits and to live our lives in a way that is pleasing to you. In Jesus' name, Amen.

3.

Growing Up and Moving On

CONTEXT

Suitable for the beginning of term (and could also be adapted as a final reflection for the close of the school year in June).

YOU WILL NEED

A small child's woolly pullover or coat, a very easy reading book, a baby's bottle, some rusks or other baby food and a cuddly toy in a baby bag or child's small rucksack.

Start off by saying how excited you are to be in school today and that you spent a long time trying to work out what you might need for the day.

You had to make sure that you had something to keep you warm (produce woolly pullover or coat), something to eat and drink (produce bottle and rusks) and something to do (the book). Say that you've also brought your favourite cuddly toy as it has always gone everywhere with you.

Ask the children if there is anything about this that doesn't appear quite right. They will (hopefully) tell you that the clothes are too small, that you're past the stage of baby food and that you should be able to cope with much more difficult reading books by now.

19

Explore this further and ask them to imagine how silly it would be if we all stayed at the same stage and still wore the clothes and ate the food we had as babies. Discuss how we all need to move on and experience new things and how exciting that can be.

Ask a few of the children to come up with suggestions of things they can do now that they couldn't do when they were younger. Ask some of the older children what they are looking forward to as they get older.

Growing up and learning new skills is what school is all about and what makes each stage of our lives so exciting. As children we learn lots of Bible stories about Jesus and the wonderful things that he did, but as we get older we see things a bit differently and we try more and more to follow his example and share his love and kindness with others.

CLOSING PRAYER OUTLINE

Our loving Father, we thank you that you are with us as we journey through life. Bless each one of us here and guide us in everything we do, say and think today and every day, that as we grow, you will help us become more and more like Jesus, in whose name we pray. Amen.

4.
A Basket of Fruit

CONTEXT
This works best in the autumn around harvest time, when many churches and traditions acknowledge the earth's resources.

YOU WILL NEED
A basket of assorted fruit from different countries e.g. apples, pears, a pineapple, a bunch of grapes, a bunch of bananas, a mango, peaches and a coconut. This is visually very attractive and a colourful start to the assembly.

Begin by admiring all the wonderful types fruit from all over the world and engage some of the children by asking them what kinds of fruit they like best or what fruit they may have brought to school in their lunchboxes that day.

Fruit and people are alike in lots of ways! Ask the children if they can think of any ways in which that might be the case.

Use the fruit in the basket to illustrate the following:
- Some people like to keep themselves to themselves [hold up a solitary fruit e.g. mango]
- Others like to go around in pairs [hold up two pears]
- While other people just love to go around in groups [hold up a bunch of bananas]

- Some people are very soft and delicate and bruise easily [hold up a peach]
- While others are as tough as nails [hold up a coconut]
- Some people we meet have always lived here [hold up an apple]
- But others have come to live here from somewhere else [hold up a pineapple].

So people and fruit can be very alike, even though we mightn't realise it! Wouldn't the basket look much less interesting if it were only full of one kind of fruit? The same goes for people: the world would be a very dull place indeed if we were all the same.

CLOSING PRAYER OUTLINE

Thank you, God our Father, for the wonder and the beauty of the world in which we live. During this season of harvest, we are especially grateful for the food we eat and the people who have worked hard to provide it for us, often in far-off places. We thank you, too, for every person that you have made, for our special place in your world and for all that we can learn from one another. Amen.

5.
Harvest From a Matchbox

CONTEXT

This very simple talk is ideal for autumn, when people are thinking about harvest. It is useful to illustrate a number of themes, like small beginnings and the yield that can result from a simple individual gesture.

YOU WILL NEED

A loaf of bread and a matchbox filled with grains of wheat or grass seed.

Ask the children if any of them had toast for breakfast before coming to school today. Draw their attention to the fact that bread is such an ordinary thing that very often we eat it without thinking a whole lot about it. In fact, every loaf of bread started out just as a sheaf of wheat in a field.

Say that you'd like to tell them the story of an American minister by the name of Clifton Robinson, who one year decided to do a little experiment. He took a matchbox [just like this one] and he packed it full of wheat seeds, finding that it took about 360 seeds to fill it. Then he planted them in the ground and waited to see what would happen.

When that crop had grown, he set the seed aside for sowing the next year and he did the same thing for six years. By that time, the 360 grains of wheat that had fitted into one matchbox had developed into a harvest covering 2,666 acres.

That sixth year, the harvest yielded 66,560 bushels of corn – enough to make 2,282,000 loaves of bread [just like this one]. Now that may be hard to imagine, but if you'd put those loaves end to end, they would have stretched for about 150 miles, or roughly from Dublin to Galway! That is a lot of bread!

All that from one little matchbox full of seed … and of course, someone to plant it.

Ask the children what they might have learnt from this. Hopefully, some suggestions will include not taking things for granted and being thankful for the food we eat. Incorporate their answers into your conclusion and also draw the children's attention to the immense amount of good that can come from the actions of one individual. Remind them that we are also part of God's creation and that we play a vital role in the care of the world in which we live.

CLOSING PRAYER OUTLINE
Father God, you provide us with the food we need to nourish our minds and our bodies. Let us never take what we have for granted but always give thanks to you for the ways in which you give us all we need. Enable us, also, to live lives that yield good fruit and make us a blessing to our world. In Jesus' name, Amen.

6.
Just the Seeds

CONTEXT
This talk can be used during the season of harvest, but to equally good effect at the start of the new school year or even in January when the post-Christmas activities resume. It is based on a story by an unknown author.

YOU WILL NEED
No equipment at all, except for an outline of the story.

Once upon a time, many years ago, a pilgrim set out on a journey in search of peace, joy and love.

The pilgrim's journey took him through landscapes that were not always happy ones. He saw people quarrelling and fighting. He saw people building walls to separate themselves from others. He saw sickness and sadness, loneliness and despair. He wandered for many miles and as time went on, as you can imagine, he became footsore and weary, not only from all the walking but also from all the trouble that he saw along the way.

Then one day, he came across a little cottage by the roadside. Something about this little house caught his attention. Through the windows, the traveller could see lights on and, filled with curiosity, he decided to go inside.

Inside the cottage was a little shop and behind the counter there stood a shopkeeper who greeted the pilgrim and asked him in a warm and kindly voice, 'What would you like?'
'What do you stock?,' asked the traveller. 'Oh, we have everything here that you most desire,' replied the shopkeeper. 'Just tell me what you long for most.'

The pilgrim hardly knew where to start. 'Well, I want peace in my family, in my home country and in the world. I want to make something good of my life. I want those who are sick to be well and those who are lonely to have friends. I want anyone who is hungry to have plenty to eat and I want every child born on this planet today to be able to go to school and get a proper education. I want everyone on earth to live in freedom and I want this world to be a kingdom of love.' He stopped speaking while he had a quick look at his shopping list to see if he might have left something out.

Gently, the shopkeeper spoke. 'I'm so sorry,' came the quiet reply. 'I should have explained. We don't supply the fruits here. We only supply the seeds.'

Explain to the children that we can want all kinds of wonderful things to happen in our world, but that it is up to us to do our bit to bring them about. We can't expect things to happen 'just like that' or on their own. We are all part of this world and it is only by everyone in it doing his or her part, that we can make things better for us all.

CLOSING PRAYER OUTLINE
Loving Father, show us how to use our lives and all that we have and are to make this world a happier and a better place for us all. Amen.

7.
The Story of
Johnny Appleseed

CONTEXT
This is an adaptation of the American legend of Johnny Appleseed. It is most suitable for the autumn, when many traditions are celebrating the world around them.

YOU WILL NEED
A small saucepan and an apple.

Ask the children if anyone has ever heard the story of a man by the name of Jonathan Chapman. No? Well then, the time has come to tell them his story.

Our story begins in the American state of Massachusetts in the year 1774, when a baby was born by the name of Jonathan Chapman. As a boy, Johnny was mad about the outdoors and used to go off on long walks in the countryside looking for birds and flowers. He was always very interested in any animals he met along the way and soon gained the reputation for being a kindly and gentle soul. He lived a very simple life, with just the clothes he stood up in; and some pictures in American storybooks show him with a saucepan on his head as he travelled about in his bare feet, camping and cooking out of doors.

The reason why Johnny became so well known was because of one particular thing that he did as he wandered through the hills and woods. He realised that with all the new settlers coming to live in the country (America was still a very young country back then), there would be a great need for food. So he went about planting apple seeds and it is thanks to him that nowadays there are so many huge apple orchards throughout the states of Ohio, Pennsylvania, Kentucky, Illinois and Indiana. News of this unusual man spread far and wide and he came to be known in America as Johnny Appleseed.

Not many people have ever heard of Jonathan Chapman, but most of the English-speaking world would be familiar with the name of Johnny Appleseed and his travels around America, planting the seeds that would become the ancestors of the fruit trees that still grow there today.

Autumn is a time when we celebrate the harvest and all the wonderful things which nature produces for us to use and enjoy. It is also a time when we appreciate the time and the care that go into the things we so often take for granted. Encourage the children, the next time they eat an apple, to save the seeds and see what they become in the days and months ahead.

CLOSING PRAYER OUTLINE
For the fruits of his creation, for his gifts to every nation, for the ploughing, sowing, reaping, silent growth while we are sleeping, future needs in earth's safe keeping, thanks be to God. Amen.

8.
Guess Who?

CONTEXT
This is a talk for Hallowe'en.

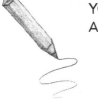

YOU WILL NEED
A mask.

Ask the children if they are going to dress up in costume this Hallowe'en. Ask them if they have made any special preparations or have any plans to do anything particular that day.

Then move on to ask them if they know how Hallowe'en came about. Some of the children may know that it is a very old tradition. Other children may talk of superstitions and other elements which have come to be associated with Hallowe'en over the years.

Explain that Hallowe'en is very old indeed and goes back to a time long ago when people thought differently about the world. At that time there was no electricity and they would have lived in a much darker world. Yes, there would have been candles and firelight, but when the days grew shorter like they have done over the past few weeks, people at that time would have spent a lot more time in the dark. As we know, the dark can sometimes be a scary place and you can start to imagine that all kinds of things might be going on in places you cannot see.

People thought especially about the spirit world and believed that there were spirits, both good and bad, all around them. It is thought that in order to scare off the bad spirits, people used to wear frightening masks and dance about making scary noises so that the bad spirits would leave them alone and disappear.

Of course, as time went on, people began to think differently about the world we inhabit. Now we have lots of light, even in the depth of winter, and we have come to understand more about how the world works. But that doesn't stop us from dressing up and having fun and many people like taking part in an ancient tradition, even if that tradition has undergone many changes over the centuries.

Hallowe'en is one of a number of things that happen at this time of year to remind us of the importance of light. We change the clocks each year, we dress up and go out from house to house at night and very soon we'll be thinking about the other kind of light that comes at Christmas. Not just the twinkly sort that we see on trees, but the kind of inner light that means understanding and which comes to us in Jesus.

CLOSING PRAYER OUTLINE
Our loving Father, over these dark winter days, bring us your light in our hearts and help us to understand more about your Son Jesus, in whose name we pray. Amen.

9.
Remembrance

CONTEXT

This talk can be used very effectively during the month of November, when many traditions focus on those who have died. In some traditions, there is a focus on the loss of life through conflict while elsewhere, people's thoughts are often focused on family and friends who have passed on over the years.

YOU WILL NEED

A selection of greeting cards marking a range of situations, occasions or rites of passage. Your selection might include any or all of the following: wedding anniversary, birth of a baby, new job, congratulations, sympathy, bat/barmitzvah, Fathers' Day, First Communion, confirmation, moving house, get well. Include one sympathy card amongst them.

Show the children the card(s) and spend a few moments exploring the reasons why people send each other cards. These reasons may include showing the other person that you care, that you are pleased for them and that you want to share in their joy.

Ask them if there is any card that is different from the others. Gradually draw the conversation towards the sympathy card, which is the only one to express sadness. Explore with the children what sending a card like this might mean to the recipient and to the sender. Some suggestions might include showing that the sender cares and is aware of the pain and sadness that the other person is experiencing, and giving comfort to the recipient, who will know that s/he has been remembered and that someone is thinking of them.

Explain that this is the time of year when many people are remembering those who have died. In churches and communities, people do this in many different ways: through special Masses, services or community gatherings. Stress that while remembering can sometimes be sad, it can also be a time of great thanksgiving as we remember the happiness that others have brought us through their lives and all that we have gained from them.

CLOSING PRAYER OUTLINE

Loving Father, sometimes we feel sad remembering those who have died. Teach us how to remember them with gratitude and to be thankful for all the happy memories that we still enjoy. In the name of Jesus, we pray. Amen.

10.
Counting Our Blessings

CONTEXT

This talk relates to Thanksgiving, an American holiday during which families share the blessings they have experienced in the previous twelve months. In some homes, five kernels of corn are placed beside each table setting and those present take it in turns to speak. Tradition has it that during the lean years of the early American settlements, there were periods of severe deprivation when food had to be strictly rationed. The 'ration' of five kernels of corn has become a symbol of the hardship, perseverance and courage of those early days.

YOU WILL NEED

For a large assembly, five kernels of corn for your own individual use; for a smaller group of up to fifteen children, try to have enough to give everyone present five kernels each. In either case, a flipchart and a marker will be helpful to record the children's responses.

Give a brief introduction to the celebration of Thanksgiving before introducing the kernels of corn.

This is a very simple but effective talk, revolving around what we think are the very special ways in which God has blessed our lives over recent months. It can be as long or as short as you wish to make it and you can take your lead from the suggestions made by those present.

CLOSING PRAYER OUTLINE
Draw all of the responses together in a closing prayer that reflects the breadth and variety of what has been said.

... For these and all your blessings to us and to all your people, we give you our thanks and praise. In the name of Jesus, we pray. Amen.

PART 2
ADVENT
CHRISTMAS
HANUKKAH

11.
Preparing For Christmas

CONTEXT
This is a Moravian tradition associated with the first Sunday in Advent (the fourth Sunday before Christmas), but it could be used in an assembly at any time during December in the run-up to Christmas.

YOU WILL NEED
An orange (with something to stand it up in like an egg cup or a napkin ring), enough red ribbon to circle the orange at its widest point in the middle and a pin to secure it), a small candle (about half an inch diameter and about four inches high), four cocktail sticks and an assortments of small sweets or dried fruit and some matches. The orange should have a hole cut out of the top of it to make it easier to push the candle in.

Say that one of the most exciting things about Christmas is the way in which many of the traditions we associate with it have come from other parts of the world and that you would like to share one such example with them today.

This is a Moravian tradition that began in Germany in 1747. A man leading a service in a Moravian church gave a candle with a red ribbon tied around it to every child in the congregation to show them how the birth of Christ lights a flame in every heart. The Moravians took this tradition all over the world and other people in other places have added on other little bits and pieces to give us today what has come to be called a Christingle.

Ask for a volunteer to help you put the Christingle together and say that this is something that they can all make for their own homes at some stage before Christmas. Invite suggestions as to the meaning as you go along.

The orange represents the world and the red ribbon around the middle is the blood of Christ who died for us all. The dried fruit represents the world's resources and a selection of the fruit/sweets is pushed on to the cocktail sticks, which are then pushed into the orange to represent the four compass points, north, south, east and west. The candle, which stands for the light of the world, is put in last and can then be lit.

CLOSING PRAYER OUTLINE
O God our Father, this Christmas, may the world know the goodness of God's creation, may the world taste the good fruits of the Spirit and may the world see the light of Christ. Amen.

12.
Babushka

CONTEXT

This is an interactive adaptation of the Russian folktale and is ideal for any day coming up to Christmas. Use volunteers from the younger classes to hold up the props as you are relating the story. It is both thought-provoking and funny.

YOU WILL NEED

A duster, a large star, a silver circle (to represent a halo), three cardboard crowns covered in silver or gold foil, a stuffed camel, a large letter Z (to represent sleep), a toy doll, a small blanket, a small bottle, a handkerchief, a walking stick, a stuffed lamb and a toy donkey.

Distribute the props at random and ask those involved to listen out for any part of the story that might need the item that they are holding in their hands.

The story starts with Babushka sitting at home doing her housework. She was a very particular woman and liked to keep her home as neat as a new pin. Some people said that it kept her from thinking about the little baby boy she had who had died, because she always seemed to be a little sad.

This particular night she was so busy polishing and tidying that she didn't notice a rather unusual star had popped up and was now shining through her window. She shooed away an angel who had come to bring her some very important news. 'You'll have to wipe your feet if you want to come in here,' she declared and the angel disappeared.

Babushka continued on with her polishing and tidying until she was disturbed by some loud knocking at the door. There on the doorstep stood three kings with shiny crowns.

'We're kings,' they said, 'And we're on our way to find a baby. Would you like to come along?' 'I haven't got time for that sort of thing,' said Babushka. 'I have my washing up and ironing still to do.' And then she saw the camels out in her garden. 'Get out! Get out!' she cried, all of a fluster, still holding her duster. The kings and the camels went off and Babushka, worn out with all the excitement, decided to have a little snooze. And while she was sleeping, she saw in her dreams a little baby in a stable, wrapped in nothing but swaddling clothes. A star shone through the window and woke her up. 'My goodness,' she said. 'That's not right! A baby should have nice warm blanket to sleep in! I must set off at once and find this baby.'

She found a little basket and put a warm blanket in it, a toy doll that had once belonged to her little boy and a small bottle of ginger cordial and trotted off down the road. She hadn't gone far when she met a woman and her little daughter who was sobbing into her handkerchief. 'We were rushing to see the new baby,' said her mother, 'but we have dropped her little doll somewhere in the snow.' 'Here,' said Babushka, taking the toy doll out of her basket, 'take this with my love.' The little girl was thrilled, wiped her eyes and Babushka continued on her way.

Not much later, Babushka met an elderly lady on a stick. 'I'm on my way to see the new baby,' she said, 'but my legs are aching with the cold and tiredness.' 'Here,' said Babushka, giving the old woman the bottle of ginger cordial she had in her basket, 'this may help to ease the pain. Take it with my love.' And on she went.

A little further on, she met a shepherd boy carrying a lamb. 'I couldn't keep up with the others', he said with his teeth chattering. 'I want so badly to give this to the new baby king.' So Babushka took the blanket, the last item in the basket. Wrapping it around his shoulders she said to the boy, 'Take this with my love' and the boy accepted it gladly.

But then as Babushka arrived in the town, she realised that her basket was completely empty. 'Well, that's useless!' she said to herself. 'Now I have nothing to give the baby,' and she turned to walk back the way she had come.

Then she heard a voice calling her name. 'Babushka,' said the voice, 'please come in.' It was Mary. There in the stable was a baby sleeping, wrapped in a warm blanket with a little toy doll beside his head and the baby's father was drinking a warming glass of ginger cordial.

'But I gave all those things away!' whispered Babushka. Mary replied, 'Everything you gave away with love, you also gave to my son.' Babushka picked the baby up and held him close, and for once in her life she completely forgot about doing any cleaning at all. All the animals gathered around, including an old donkey, and the star shone brightly over them all.

CLOSING PRAYER OUTLINE
God our Father, keep our eyes open this Christmas that we may not miss the wonder of the birth of your Son Jesus. In the middle of all our preparations, help us to remember the needs of others and that in helping them, we are also serving you. Amen.

13.
Turning to Face the Light

CONTEXT

This works particularly well when the clocks go back at the end of October, but it is also suitable for the run-up to the Christmas holidays when it can be used to illustrate the theme of Jesus as the Light of the World.

YOU WILL NEED

A solar-powered calculator.

Introduce the theme by noting how short the days have become recently and compare the days now with those during the height of the summer months.

Ask the children for suggestions of things they need to do at this time of year when there is less light, things that they don't need to do in the summer. For example, some children may own a reflective jacket, others may have luminous armbands, others may have extra lights on their bicycles.

Stress that light is very important in all our lives. Then explain that your solar-powered calculator is, of course, completely useless unless there is light. Exaggerate this a little and ask a child to take the calculator over towards a nearby window or over to a light bulb, do a simple calculation on it and to show you the result. Then you can tell the children that once you have finished using it, you can slip it back into its little pouch or bag and that it stops working straight away.

The calculator needs light in order to be able to work properly. The very same can be said of people. We need light to see, so that we don't fall over things in the dark. But we also need another kind of light and that is the light inside us. This is the light that helps us to see and to understand the ways in which Jesus wants us to live our lives.

Ask the children to think of a time when they have had difficulty trying to understand something that the teacher is explaining to them. Then ask them to try and remember that feeling they got when they suddenly got the hang of it.

Jesus came into the world at Christmas to bring that kind of light, to help people understand more about God and to see things more clearly. Like the calculator, we work best when we face the light: Jesus Christ, the Light of the World.

CLOSING PRAYER OUTLINE
Father God, you sent your Son Jesus into our world of darkness to bring us light. Help us to learn to keep our eyes focused on him, that we may grow to understand more how best to live our lives. In his name we pray, Amen.

14.
God Jul!
Fröhliche Weinachten!

CONTEXT
Either Christmas or Easter, when it can be used to underline the essential unity of Christian people throughout the world. It works particularly well in a multicultural context and enables new children from other countries and backgrounds to contribute something of their own to the group.

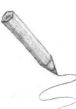

YOU WILL NEED
A flip chart and a variety of coloured markers and some examples of greetings in languages other than English to get the assembly started.

Start a few minutes beforehand, or even as the children are gathering, to write down one or two seasonal greetings in another language (the more unusual the better, to keep them guessing!)

Welcome everyone and ask if they have any idea at all what the words on the flip chart might mean. Once they have worked out what it is, you can ask anyone else in the room if they know how to say and write the same thing in another language and gradually fill up the flip chart with greetings from all over the world.

Use this as the basis for an affirmation of our world and all the variety that it contains, and stress the ways in which we can all learn so much from one another.

CLOSING PRAYER OUTLINE

Our loving Father, we thank you for the world in which we live and for all the different kinds of people we meet. Help us to understand one another better and to work to build friendships that encourage and support one another day by day. In Jesus' name, we pray, Amen.

15.
Button Marie

CONTEXT
Ideal for a Sunday after Christmas, when thoughts are moving on to the New Year. It was first used as a children's talk during the Methodist Covenant Service to illustrate God's constant love for us, but it could also be used at any other time of year to make the same point. There are several ways in which you can draw the story to a conclusion, making it very useful for a mixed-age group. It is adapted from *The Gingerbread Doll* by Susan Tews.

YOU WILL NEED
To read or memorise the story. A very attractive and interesting addition is to make a thick gingerbread doll and dress it in roughly cut fabric as an illustration. Wrap it in brown paper, tie it up with string and place it on a table to be introduced later.

The story is set in America during the Depression of the 1930s and centres on a young girl by the name of Rebecca Wilcox, whose family leave home in Illinois in a battered old truck to make the long, cold journey through the snow to a new farm in Wisconsin.

When they arrived they discovered that the new farmhouse was in a dreadful state, but Rebecca's father was determined to make the best of this new situation and set about organising his new farm. But hail destroyed much of the first year's crop and her father said that it would be a lean Christmas.

Despite this, Rebecca still hoped that she might receive the lovely porcelain doll that she had seen in a toyshop in town, but she said nothing. Times were so hard for the family that year, that all they could afford to give each other were tiny gifts, like walnuts and pencils wrapped up very simply in brown paper and tied with string. Rebecca and the older children tried to be excited for the younger ones, but deep down she was bitterly disappointed that there was no special gift for her.

Her mother saw the look on her face and said, 'I couldn't get you that doll you wanted, sweetheart, but I got to thinking. I had a bit of extra molasses so I baked you a gingerbread doll.' And with that, she went to the cupboard and took out a brown paper parcel tied with string and gave it to her. [Here you might unwrap the doll you have made and show it to the children.]

Mama had rolled out the dough extra thick and used a knife to cut out the shape of a girl. She'd stuck in wool for her hair and she'd stitched together pieces of cloth for her clothes and, finally, she had added three shiny buttons. Rebecca was thrilled and knew straight away what to call her: 'Button Marie,' she said with delight, 'that's her name!'

How Rebecca loved that doll. She played with her constantly, dressing her, tying her hair in braids and using a box lid as her bed. She would still have loved to have that porcelain doll, but she loved Button Marie in a way that you can never love something bought in a shop.

One day, she was playing with her doll when it slipped from her fingers and crashed to the floor. [Here, for effect, you can drop the doll.] Bits of Button Marie scattered all over the bedroom and Rebecca was devastated. She gathered up all the pieces and went to her mother to see if she could put them back together again.

'But honey,' said her mother, 'Button Marie was never meant to last forever. She was only a cookie.'

'She was NOT just a cookie,' sobbed Rebecca. 'She was a doll!' 'She was a doll because you loved her,' replied her mother. Sadly, Rebecca went away and put Button Marie's dress in a drawer.

Months passed and things began to improve on the farm. The next year there was a good harvest and the Wilcox's barn was full of hay. The house was repaired and freshly painted and that year, the slightly bigger Christmas presents were wrapped in coloured paper. Things were getting better.

Rebecca felt sure that she could never love another doll as much as she had loved Button Marie, but that year her Christmas gift was another doll, this time made out of corn husks. Some of the ladies in the village had taught Mama how to soak and bend the husks, and when she had finished making the doll, she had added in a face. Rebecca thought that the corn-husk doll was beautiful. After another year, she was given a shop-bought doll, made out of cloth, and sometimes she would put Button Marie's old dress on her, just for fun.

Then one Christmas, a few years later, Rebecca did get her porcelain doll. A beautiful doll with long chestnut-coloured ringlets and a satin and velvet dress. It was what she had always wanted and she was delighted. But she never forgot her very first doll, Button Marie, and kept her old dress, which she went on to show to her daughter and granddaughter when they got together every Christmas to make gingerbread cookies for all the members of the family. And the message she always gave them was this: 'Button Marie was made from love, and that's the part of a gingerbread doll that lasts forever.'

Points that may be raised here in conclusion:

* We get lots of presents for Christmas but we must remember that the gift is never more important than the love and the thought that goes into it.
* Now that Christmas is over, we need to remind ourselves that of all the gifts we ever receive, it is the gift of Jesus that is the most important one of all, and that lasts a lot longer. Christmas has come and gone but what it means lives on.
* Life is full of ups and downs, but through it all, God's love for us remains constant and secure.

CLOSING PRAYER OUTLINE
For your love which never leaves us and stays with us throughout our lives, both through good times and bad, we thank you, loving Father. Amen.

16.
Anything Missing?

CONTEXT
This was first used on Christmas Day as part of a morning service, but it would be equally effective any time close to the end of Advent. It takes a bit of planning, so allow for that well in advance.

YOU WILL NEED
About seven cardboard boxes, each fitting easily inside the next one; wrapping paper; adhesive tape; seven jumbo-sized luggage labels; and a small religious decoration depicting Jesus, which can be wrapped and placed inside the smallest box. By the time you meet the children, most of the work will already have been done.

Start with the small symbol or decoration. Wrap it up and place it in the smallest box, which you then wrap up like a present. Stick a label with the words 'ANYTHING MISSING?' on it. Then place this box inside the next box wrap it up, affix another label with another Christmassy, but frivolous word on it (e.g. crackers) and put it inside the next box. Continue until you have used up all the boxes and labels.

The talk begins with what seems to be one enormous Christmas present sitting on the table with a label attached. Gather the children around and say that you're going to have great fun unwrapping this Christmas present today and that while you're doing it, you're going to chat about some of the really important things to do with Christmas. Draw their attention to the label and say that to start things off, you'd like someone to say something about what's on the label. Once you've done that, get one of the children to unwrap the present ... only to discover another one inside.

Ask another child to talk about what's on this next label and another one to unwrap it. Keep going until you reach the last box (with the decoration inside and the 'ANYTHING MISSING?' label on the outside). Pause there for a moment, think back over all the things that you've spoken about and ask them to think hard to see if there is anything they might have forgotten in all the excitement.

Someone may, hopefully, suggest Jesus. Ask them to unwrap the last box and to reveal what has been hidden inside. The message should be clear: that we can be so caught up in the silliness and the busyness of Christmas that we can sometimes forget what it is that is really at the centre of it all.

CLOSING PRAYER OUTLINE
God our loving Father, in all the excitement of Christmas, help us to remember what the centre of this special time is really all about. In the midst of all our happiness, give us that deeper joy which comes from knowing that you have loved us enough to send Jesus into our world to show us the things that are really important in our lives. In his name we pray. Amen.

17.
Celebrating Hanukkah

CONTEXT
Suitable for any day during Hanukkah, which falls at some point in December. It is useful in terms of broadening the children's understanding of Jewish history and culture and helps to fill in some of the background to the story of Jesus.

YOU WILL NEED
A nine-branch brass candlestick (a *hanukkiah*) or one made out of dough or clay, eight thin candles and some matches.

Explain to the children that the story you are about to share with them is a story that many Jewish children will be hearing during this very special festival of Hanukkah.

Over 2,000 years ago, the Jewish people lived in a small country called Judah. They were ruled over by a Greek king called Antiochus, who was a reasonable sort of man and let the Jews live their lives in peace.

One of the things that the Jews did was to celebrate festivals in a special way, and for these they would travel to the Temple in Jerusalem. Inside the temple there was a courtyard. It was here that the Jews gathered to give offerings to God and to join in prayers led by the High Priest. Antiochus allowed the Jewish people to do these things because he knew that these traditions were important to them.

But one day, king Antiochus died. His son, Antiochus IV, was crowned king in his place, but he was a very different kind of king. He hated the Jewish people and made a new law that said that if they didn't give up all their religious practices and become Greeks, they would die. He got his men to break into the temple, where they smashed up all the Jewish statues and furniture and burnt all their holy books. Then he decided to send his army all over the country to make people obey him, and off they went.

A group of Antiochus's soldiers arrived in a small town called Modin with a Greek statue and demanded that all the people living there give up their Jewish beliefs and worship it instead. The villagers were horrified. A village elder, Mattathias, stepped forward and said, 'We will not do what you ask.' 'Then I shall have to kill you on the king's orders,' replied the officer in charge. There was a scuffle. A terrified villager bent down to worship the statue. Mattathias rushed at him and brought the statue to the ground, while his five sons attacked the soldiers. The men of the village then decided to prepare for battle and ran off into the hills to get ready.

For several months the men held out in the hills but one sad day, Mattathias died and handed over the responsibility of the fighting to his son. By now, Antiochus VI knew full well what was going on and sent a force of 2,000 men to crush the Jews for once and for all. But the Jews were waiting and fought back with rocks and stones, and despite the efforts of Antiochus and his vast army of trained soldiers, the Jewish people just could not be beaten.

After some time, when the enemy had been overcome, the Jewish people made their way back into Jerusalem, feeling that the time had come for them to rebuild their lives. But when they got there, they found the temple in a terrible state. The courtyard was overgrown and there were Greek statues everywhere. The Jews were horrified. Then Judah, one Mattathias's sons, took charge. Together they cleaned the temple, rebuilt the altar and went to light the menorah (the seven-branch candlestick) which was a very important part of their tradition. To their alarm, they discovered that there was only enough oil for it to last one day. Yet, to everyone's amazement, the light lasted for a full eight days. So they did what a lot of people would have done after a success in battle and after the relief of being able to use their temple once again: they threw a party!

It is for this reason that during Hanukkah, Jewish people have a nine-branch candlestick (a *hanukkiah*), which they light gradually over the eight days using the *shamash*, or servant candle, which is the central candle. They will also give each other gifts, play games and enjoy this very special part of their year. The word 'Hanukkah' means dedication in Hebrew and reminds them, and now us, of the new start which the people of Judah enjoyed as they rebuilt and rededicated their temple to God.

CLOSING PRAYER OUTLINE
O God, you have guided and protected your people since earliest times. Help us always to remember your goodness and kindness and to give you our thanks and praise. Amen.

18.
Habari Gani?
The Story of Kwanzaa

CONTEXT

The festival of Kwanzaa originated in the United States in 1966 and is a non-religious celebration of African-American culture. The name Kwanzaa is derived from a Swahili word meaning 'first fruits' and the celebrations start on 26 December and last for seven days. Each day highlights one of the universal principles or beliefs (known as the Nguzo Saba) common to those of African-American heritage, and each of these cultural beliefs is celebrated in the context of the family and the community. This talk is best used at some point during the month of December.

YOU WILL NEED

A *kinara* candlestick (or equivalent), which should be able to hold seven candles. You will also need three red candles, three green candles and one black candle. The colours of these candles are significant: the black is for the face of the African people; the red is for the ways in which Africa has suffered in the past and green symbolises hope for the future. One candle is lit every day as the celebrations continue throughout the week. If you are using this talk on one occasion only, you will light all seven as you move through your talk.

Start the talk by asking the children to name some of the celebrations they mark each year. This will lead very naturally on to the ways in which other people and cultures mark special events around the world.

Outline very briefly the background to Kwanzaa and then invite seven individual children to light the candles as you explain what they represent. This would be particularly meaningful in a multi-racial context. Depending on the amount of time you have available, you may also like to ask for examples from the other children as to how these principles might work in their lives.

Light the central candle (black) as you focus on the first principle of **Umoja** (unity).
This refers to the strength of the family and to the building up of a strong community.

The second candle (red) represents **Kujichagulia** (determination). This refers to the ability to stand up for oneself and to taking responsibility for one's own future.

The third candle (green) stands for **Ujima** (working together).
This stresses the idea that people should help one another and share each other's burdens.

The fourth candle (red) focuses on **Ujamaa** (supporting African-American business).
This is rather like our own Guaranteed Irish campaign and focuses on encouraging local enterprise and initiative.

The fifth candle (green) stands for **Nia** (purpose).
This relates to respecting and honouring those who have gone before us.

The sixth candle (red) represents **Kuumba** (creativity). This encourages people to express themselves culturally through art and music.

The final candle (green) is lit to symbolise **Imani** (faith). This is a very general term that draws together the ideas of faith in our beliefs, as well as our hopes and dreams for the future.

You might conclude your talk by saying that once all the candles have been lit, there is a big party with lots of traditional African food, dancing and storytelling.

Finally, make the point that Kwanzaa is a festival that asks all of us to take care of each other, support each other and respect ourselves. Even though it is an African-American celebration, the ideas behind it are ones that we should all try to remember in our daily lives.

CLOSING PRAYER OUTLINE
O God our Father, we thank you for all that we can learn from other people and for all that we share with those from different backgrounds. During this season of celebration, help us remember what is truly important in our lives and in the year ahead may we do what we can to be a blessing to our families, our communities and to our world. Amen.

19.
Christmas Traditions

CONTEXT
Any time coming up to the Christmas holidays, as an address to the children as part of a Christmas Eve service or on Christmas Day itself. This is a very simple, attractive and informative talk and can be adapted to include a whole range of other traditions from further afield.

YOU WILL NEED
A selection of traditional Christmas items, e.g. a mince pie, tinsel, a striped candy cane and a piece of holly. You will also need to have done a little bit of research into whatever decorations and/or symbols you have decided to use.

Ask the children what comes into their minds when they think of Christmas and have a brief discussion about some of the traditions they enjoy in their families and homes.

Move on to draw their attention to the fact that while we do lots of wonderful things at Christmas, sometimes we don't think very much about how those traditions all started off in the first place.

Say that today you're going to share with them some of the stories and legends that have grown up around a few of the things we see and use at Christmas time. Some examples might include the following:

- Tinsel – the story of the Holy Family on the run from Egypt and the web which a spider wove over the entrance to where they were hiding to escape the soldiers looking for them.
- Mince pie – representing the crib and the blanket, the traditional three spices in the mince meat symbolise the three kings.
- Candy cane – a shepherd's crook, an inverted 'J' for Jesus and the red representing the blood shed for his people.
- Holly – evergreen, crown of thorns, red berries reminding us of the sacrifice of Jesus and his everlasting love for us all.

Close by saying that all of these stories are attempts that people have made over hundreds of years to explain the most wonderful event of all: the story of the birth of Jesus at Christmas.

CLOSING PRAYER OUTLINE
God, our Father, thank you for all the things around us at Christmas which remind us of you and of your Son Jesus, whose birth we celebrate and who came to bring us life, light and hope. In his name we pray. Amen.

20.
Crisis On Christmas Eve

CONTEXT
This is suitable for any time coming up to Christmas and is an adapted version of the story of the origin of the carol 'Silent Night'.

YOU WILL NEED
Either a copy of the story to read, or to have already memorised it. If you can arrange for someone to accompany the children on the guitar, it makes for a very simple but effective conclusion.

The story starts on Christmas Eve in the Austrian village of Oberndorf, in the year 1818. The local townspeople and others from the surrounding villages were busily preparing for one of the highlights of the whole year – the Christmas Eve Mass, to be held in the Church of St Nicholas. But during the final choir practice that afternoon, the organ had stopped working and the organist, Franz Gruber, had to send the children home, telling them that they would not be needed that night because they could not sing without the proper organ accompaniment.

So the children left and Franz Gruber trudged home through the thick snow, all of them disappointed and downhearted at the thought of no proper Christmas music. When the priest,

Father Joseph Mohr, heard the news, he immediately set about lengthening his sermon to fill in some of the space left by the lack of music, but nothing came to him … until the words of a simple song came into his head. He quickly composed six verses and rushed off to the home of Franz Gruber and his family. 'Quickly!' said Father Joseph, 'Can you compose a simple tune to these words for the Mass tonight?' 'I'll try my best,' said Herr Gruber, and asked his sons to let the choir know that they would be needed after all and to turn up early at the church that evening.

When everyone had gathered, Father Mohr explained to the singers that a new song had been composed for the Mass and that he would have to accompany it with a guitar because the organ was still not working. And so it was that 'Silent Night' was born, first sung all those years ago to the gentle chords of a guitar.

It is very effective if the assembly can conclude with the singing of the carol to guitar accompaniment, especially if the guitarist is one of the children.

(Some versions of this story attribute the organ breakdown to the activities of a mouse chewing through the organ pipes. An innovative variation on the tale might be to tell it from the perspective of the mouse.)

CLOSING PRAYER OUTLINE

Dear Father, as we celebrate this season of Christmas, we thank you for the ways in which different people have felt inspired to express the wonder of the birth of Jesus in poetry and song, that we may understand more of your love and care for us. Amen.

PART 3
NEW YEAR
LENT
EASTER
PENTECOST
SUMMER

21.
Where Have You Seen This Before?

CONTEXT

This talk can be used in a variety of contexts to convey a whole range of messages. It could be adapted for use to illustrate the opportunity for a fresh start that comes to us every year in the birth of Jesus, at the start of a new year or on those occasions when you might like to focus on the environment, but it ties in particularly well with the theme of new life at Easter.

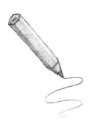

YOU WILL NEED

One or more items made from recycled materials. Examples might include a bag made out of recycled juice cartons, a notebook which used to be a car tyre, or a toy made out of bits of old wire.

This very simple and easy talk focuses on the issue of recycling. Ask the children if they do any recycling at home. Hopefully there will be lots of suggestions. Expand on this to say that recycling is becoming more and more common nowadays as people are beginning to realise how important it is to look after our world more carefully.

Show the children what you have brought and ask them to guess what it might have been before it came to look like it does now. Once you have done that, move on to talk about what a good thing it is to be able to make something new and different out of something else. Essentially, whoever made this item has created something new.

Jesus said, 'Behold I am making something new!' That new thing is us. When we say that we are sorry about the bad things we have done or sorry about the things we should have done, but haven't, Jesus tells us that we are forgiven and encourages us to start all over again and to try and do better the next time.

So, with the arrival of Jesus in our lives, we get a chance to recycle ourselves, to start again and to try and do things better the next time around. Even when we get a bit tired and worn out, even when we make mistakes or run out of energy or feel a bit of a flop, we are given the chance of a new start. Jesus forgives us our sins and gives us all a second chance.

CLOSING PRAYER OUTLINE
Our loving Father, we thank you that, through your forgiveness, we have the opportunity of a fresh start. Help us to try and learn from the lessons of the past, to start afresh and to live more and more like Jesus day by day. In his name we pray. Amen.

22.
Time For a Check-Up

CONTEXT
This is an excellent introduction to the season of Lent, but it could also be used at the start of a new year.

YOU WILL NEED
Several items out of a child's doctor's kit, like a stethoscope, a 'light' to shine in someone's ear, a pretend syringe to give someone an injection and a lollipop stick to check for tonsillitis. A white lab coat or an x-ray smock would be a nice touch if you can manage it, as would a packet of jellies to be handed out as 'tablets' when the kids leave the 'surgery'.

Introduce the theme by saying that when we're sick we have to go and see a doctor. Ask for a show of hands as to who has ever been to a doctor. See if any of them can tell you what kinds of things they might expect to happen in a doctor's surgery.

Ask for one or more volunteers to come up while you check them out for a variety of illnesses and as you are examining them you can ask them a whole range of other questions about how well they are sleeping at the moment, what they had for breakfast today, if they are in any pain and so on. This can be great fun and can be used to great effect.

When you have examined the volunteers and given them a clean bill of health, you can say how important it is to keep an eye on our health so that if we have a little problem of any kind it can be dealt with and we can be sure that it won't get out of control because that could be very serious indeed.

Move on to suggest that this is the time of year when we do another kind of check-up. Not a medical check-up like the one we've just done, but another kind that can help us keep us on the right track with our relationship with God.

Lent is a bit like going to the doctor's. It is a time when we stop and think a bit more about ourselves and how we are getting along. It's a time when we admit that we have done things that maybe we shouldn't have, we try to improve and to do things better – not only for ourselves but for those around us too. A lot of people will do something a bit different during Lent, like read the Bible more, try to give up something they enjoy or take on something extra which they feel might help others. But whatever we do, the idea is still the same: to spend time thinking about our spiritual health and keeping in good shape for God.

CLOSING PRAYER OUTLINE

Help us, O God, to use this special time to think about the ways in which we can do things in a better way and be a real blessing to your world. In the name of Jesus, Amen.

23.
What Are You Giving Up For Lent?

CONTEXT

Any time before or during the first week of Lent. It is perhaps best aimed at the 8–12 age group, but it can be simplified for younger children, too.

YOU WILL NEED

Either a flip chart and a marker (for a larger group) or a number of strips of blank card in three colours and Blu-Tack to stick them to a wall or board. You will also need a couple of older volunteers with reasonably good writing skills to help you.

Start by asking the children what they have decided to give up for Lent and have one of the volunteers jot down some of the suggestions on pieces of card of the same colour and display them nearby. Suggestions may include chocolate, sweets, television, less time on the computer and so on.

Then ask them another question: why are they doing this? Ask another volunteer to write down the reasons on a card of a different colour and to display them alongside the first responses. Suggestions may include health reasons, the opportunity to develop other interests and to socialise more.

Move on to ask a third question: can they think of any other things that people might try to give up for Lent that can't be seen? Things that people might try to stop doing because they know they are unhelpful to themselves or to others? This may take a little longer, but suggestions may include stopping gossiping, telling lies or finding fault with people. These can be recorded on card of a third colour and added to the display.

Finally ask the children what they might start doing during Lent that would be helpful to others. This part will include some overlap with the previous section, but it may also open up a discussion about donating pocket money to a worthy cause, sponsorship, doing something a bit extra to help someone else and so on. These can also be recorded and displayed.

Conclude by saying that Lent is a time when we can give things up just for ourselves, maybe to prove that we can do it; that Lent can also be a time when we can stop some of our bad habits and try to improve; and that Lent can be a time when we think less about ourselves and focus more on the needs of others, both close to home and further away.

CLOSING PRAYER OUTLINE
Loving Father, help us to think hard about why we do the things we do. Guide us in our thoughts and in our actions this Lent that we may always try to do your will. Amen.

24.
Food For Thought

CONTEXT

This was first used during Lent, when the focus was on Jesus as the Bread of Life. It can also be used effectively in conjunction with the story of the temptation in the wilderness and with the song 'Seek Ye First the Kingdom of God'.

YOU WILL NEED

A large picture of a pretzel, which can be seen clearly from a distance, and a small packet of pretzels with enough to hand out one to each of the children. If you are feeling really adventurous, you might like to make a batch at home and bring them in wrapped in clear plastic bags for the children to take away.

Ask the children if they know what the picture is of. Some will already know and you may like to pass the packet around at this point so that everyone can have a nibble. Then draw the children's attention to the pretzels' shape. Ask the children if they have any idea why they might be the shape they are. Explore some of their suggestions before moving on to tell them the story behind the pretzel.

The main elements of the story are as follows:

- pretzels seem to have originated in Italy hundreds of years ago
- a local priest gave them to the children in the locality as a reward for saying their prayers regularly during Lent
- the three spaces represent the Father, Son and Holy Spirit
- the cross in the middle stands for the arms crossed in prayer, hence the original name *bracchiola* which means 'little arms' in Italian.

Use the illustration to draw the children's attention to the additional truth that Jesus described himself as 'the Bread of Life'. He wants his people to gain strength and nourishment from his teachings, just as we all get nourishment from the bread that we eat every day.

CLOSING PRAYER OUTLINE

God our Father, you have taught us that people do not live by bread alone, but also by every word that comes from you. Help us this Lent to learn more about what that means for each one of us and to live out our faith simply. In the name of Jesus, Amen.

25.
The Roar of the Crowd

CONTEXT
Ideal for Palm Sunday or the days leading up to it. It could also be used to focus on other issues like peer pressure and independent thinking.

YOU WILL NEED
No equipment at all.

This quick and easy talk can be very lively and boisterous but it makes its point well.

Ask the children to imagine themselves in a variety of situations and to react appropriately. Some of these might include the following:

- Someone in your family has just had a new baby and isn't s/he lovely?
- Your football team has just scored a winning goal in extra time!
- At a pantomime, the villain has just emerged from behind a curtain!

- Your favourite football team has just missed a goal by inches!
- You're all doing a sponsored silence for charity and someone talks out loud!

Expand on this, drawing their attention to the extra energy they generated as a crowd. There is a completely different feeling in a situation where you are one of a group.

Move on to relate it to the events of Palm Sunday and Holy Week: when Jesus entered Jerusalem, the crowd was thrilled, so let's hear an enthusiastic welcome [the children respond]. They threw palm branches on the ground and were delighted that their King had arrived. But as we know, over the next few days, the mood of the people changed. They had expected someone powerful and capable of making important decisions and they became angry and annoyed [the children respond]. By the time we get to Easter, they want him to be crucified and when the moment comes for them to decide who it was that is to be killed, they shout 'Crucify him!' [children respond].

There are many things that we can learn from this about being one of a group. The first is that it can be great fun being surrounded by people who are all on the same side and who share the same interests. But a crowd can also turn nasty and then being part of a group is not so much fun at all.

CLOSING PRAYER OUTLINE
O God our Father, at Easter the crowd changed from a welcome party into an angry mob. Help us to avoid doing anything that brings dishonour to your Son, Jesus Christ. Amen.

26.
Cross Purposes

CONTEXT
This talk is ideal for the Easter season, when thoughts are focusing on the meaning of the death and the resurrection of Christ.

YOU WILL NEED
A variety of different kinds of cross, either actual or in picture form.

This is a very simple, but powerful address, designed to draw the children's attention to the many ways in which different countries and cultures have interpreted the symbol of the cross.

Some possibilities might include:

- A Celtic cross (the combination of pagan and Christian elements)
- A Georgian cross (traditionally made of vine leaves and tied with St Nino's hair)
- A St Brigid's cross (made of rushes and used as an illustration)
- A Taize cross (covered in a collage of pictures of people from around the world)

- An Orthodox cross (with several cross pieces)
- A Mennonite cross (with a central dove on a series of superimposed crosses arranged at angles to convey the activity of the Holy Spirit)
- A Salvadorean cross (with painted representations of the life of someone who may have suffered for their faith)

It might also be interesting, particularly for the children in the older classes, to design their own crosses and to present those designs as part of a follow-up assembly at a later date.

CLOSING PRAYER OUTLINE

Loving Father, the cross reminds us that your Son died for the sins of all your people throughout the world. We thank you for all that we have learnt from his example and we ask for your special guidance and blessing as we try to follow in his footsteps. In his name we pray. Amen.

27.
Decorating an Easter Tree

CONTEXT
This can be used either during the last week of term before the Easter holidays or as an address to the children during an Easter morning service.

YOU WILL NEED
Some dead branches (symbolising the death of Christ), which can be placed in a sturdy vase, and a collection of Easter decorations (representing signs of new life) to be hung on the branches. These may include:

- Decorated Easter eggs
- Palm Sunday cross with red ribbon tied in a criss-cross shape
- Some artificial flowers
- A butterfly or two
- Any other ornaments depicting young animals and/or birds
- A red egg
- Three plain crosses.

This talk can be as simple or as elaborate as you wish. You may like to include some Easter decorations from other traditions, e.g. the red egg from the Orthodox Christian Easter, which represents the blood of Christ. The butterfly, with its emergence from the cocoon, is also a very ancient symbol of the resurrection.

Alternatively, you may like to suggest that the children make the decorations themselves sometime in advance, in which case the talk will centre on their contributions and efforts to create the symbols to adorn the tree.

Either way, it is an attractive and instructive way to discuss the meaning and the symbolism of Easter.

CLOSING PRAYER OUTLINE
O God our Father, you sent your Son Jesus into our world to show us how much you love us, to teach us how to live better lives and to die on the cross. Help us to remember that out of his death springs new life and enable us to celebrate this Easter in a fresh new way, we pray. Amen.

28.
The Butterfly

CONTEXT
Any time of year, but it would be very appropriate as an illustration of the Easter story in the spring. It might be most suitable for an older age group, owing to its more reflective content. It is adapted from a well-known story by an unknown author.

YOU WILL NEED
A picture of a fully-fledged, brightly coloured butterfly (or paintings of butterflies done by the children themselves) and a blank butterfly cut-out without any colour at all.

Show the children the picture of the butterfly and make a point of stressing the beauty of the colours. Ask the children if they have ever seen a butterfly up close and get them to tell you what colour it was. Explain that you are going to tell them a story about a butterfly and that you are hoping that they might be able to work out what it means.

There was once a gardener who noticed a chrysalis hanging in his garden shed. He kept an eye on it over several days when one day, he saw that it had begun to split open. He watched it carefully and saw a head slowly emerging from the chrysalis.

For about an hour the gardener remained rooted to the spot watching as the butterfly struggled to get itself out. It was an immense task, but then, all of a sudden it was free and the butterfly slowly unfolded its wings so that they could dry out in the sun. The gardener was thrilled to see the wings turn the most beautiful colours. Then the butterfly flew away.

A year later, the same gardener noticed another butterfly chrysalis hanging in much the same place in his tool shed. Remembering how difficult it had been for the first butterfly the previous year, he decide to give the butterfly a helping hand. So he cut a little slit in the outer case, thinking that this would make life easier for the butterfly to get out. Right enough, the butterfly emerged without any struggle at all but when its wings had dried out, they were withered and weak and had no colour at all.

Ask the children if they have learnt anything from the story. There are at least two themes that you may like to explore with them. Firstly, explain that in the natural world there is a cycle of growth that is best left alone. Everything has its season. Certain things need to happen at particular times for things to develop as they should. Secondly, talk about how, sometimes, in life, there has to be an element of struggle in order for the best results to come about. It is the wriggling of the butterfly that triggers the vessels in its wings to produce the pigment for the colours. The struggle is essential for the butterfly to be what it is meant to be – a beautiful, colourful part of God's creation.

CLOSING PRAYER OUTLINE
O God our Father, we thank you for the beauty of the world around us. Help us to treat nature kindly and to be open to learn the lessons it teaches us. In the name of Jesus, Amen.

29.
Let's Go and Fly a Kite!

CONTEXT
This works best during the summer term when thoughts are beginning to turn towards the holidays. It can also be used to illustrate the significance of the Holy Spirit at Pentecost.

YOU WILL NEED
A traditional diamond-shaped kite, with a wooden frame and a string of different coloured ribbons attached.

Introduce the theme by asking if anyone has ever flown a kite. Is there anyone who owns a kite? Can s/he describe it? What is the nicest thing about kite flying? Say that you have brought along a kite to show them today for a number of very special reasons, because there is a lot that we can learn from kites about God.

First of all, consider its shape and the way that it is kept stiff by the wooden poles on the reverse. Ask the children if the shape of those wooden poles reminds them of anything. Someone may mention the fact that it looks like a cross. It is the cross that helps the kite keep its shape. The same goes for people. Jesus is the one who shapes our lives and gives us a framework within which to live.

Next, consider the tail of the kite with its coloured bows and ribbons. Ask the children to describe it. Someone may mention the fact that all the bows are different colours or that they are all attached to the same piece of string. Relate to this by talking about how there are all kinds of Christian people, but no matter what their colour, no matter what their size, they are all part of God's worldwide family and we are all travelling in the same direction together.

Lastly, ask the children what a kite needs most of all to be able to do its job properly. Hopefully, someone will suggest the wind. It is only when there is a strong enough wind that the kite can do what it is meant to do, which is to fly and flutter in the sky. After Jesus died, he sent the Holy Spirit to move amongst his people and to help them to do good things for other people. In the Bible, the Holy Spirit is described as 'a mighty rushing wind'. When we feel like making someone welcome, when we help someone in need, when we share what we have with others, these are actions prompted by the Holy Spirit, who blows through our lives like a wind and helps us to do those things that Jesus needs us to do, right here where we live.

CLOSING PRAYER OUTLINE
Loving Father, we thank you for Jesus who died on the cross to show us the way to heaven and for the Holy Spirit, which helps us and all your people to bring happiness to others. Make us more like Jesus, day by day. Amen.

30.
Off to the Seaside

CONTEXT
Any time coming up to the summer holidays.

YOU WILL NEED
A summery looking bag containing a selection of beach holiday paraphernalia, e.g. bucket, spade, swimsuit, fishing net, flippers and sun cream.

Ask the children if any of them are going on a seaside holiday this summer. No doubt they will be excited to tell you where they'll be going and you won't be short of contributions! Explore with them some of the things that people do on beaches and ask them to make some suggestions. If any of the suggestions match the items you have in your bag you can produce the relevant item as you go along.

Very often when we walk on a beach we can tell that other people have been there before us. How do we know that other people have been on the beach before we have? Ask if anyone has ever found anything on a beach that shows that there have been others here before you. Some suggestions might include a training shoe, a hat or a bottle top. Other suggestions might include things that other people have made, like sandcastles, or the marks from a volleyball game, cricket match or motorbike tracks.

Consider the footprints that people can see on the sand. Very often we can see that someone has been on the beach with a dog, with one or two children, even on horseback.
From time to time we come to a place where a river slices the beach in two and we can wonder how best to cross it. Then we notice that someone has already been across and we can see by the footprints on the far side that it was a safe place to cross and so we follow where that person has been.

All of this reminds us that we leave tracks behind us wherever we go. Not just on beaches but in our lives as we grow up and get older. And just as we rely sometimes on those who have gone before us to help us to move forward safely, so too there are others coming behind us who will need our guidance as to the right way to go as they journey through life.

CLOSING PRAYER OUTLINE
We thank you God, for the season of summer and for the opportunity to experience new places and to make new friends. As we leave school for the holidays, we ask that you will continue to be with us all and guide us in the right path. In the name of Jesus, Amen.

PART 4
ALL SEASONS

31.
The Same But Different

CONTEXT

Any time of the year and ideally in a context in which there is a uniform (e.g. PE day), when all or some of the children will be wearing the same outfit.

YOU WILL NEED

A variety of euro coins.

Start out by asking any of the children if they collect anything. Ask them why they do this and explore the idea of gathering together things that are connected in some way.

Take out your euro coins and, first of all, describe the side with the denomination on it. Compare a few coins of the same denomination that come from different countries in the euro zone. They look the same at first glance but as they children will know, they are different on the other side. Ask the children why this might be the case. Hopefully, it will emerge that each country has its own picture on the reverse side, representing something about that particular country.

We often think by looking at people who look alike on the outside that they must also be alike on the inside. Use the example of a school uniform to illustrate this. We might assume that they think and act the same way as each other or that because people are the same age they must like the same things. Of course, as human beings, there are things that we all have in common. Ask the children for examples of what those things might be. Then ask them to think of some way in which they are different from other family members or from their friends.

Explain that while God has made each of us unique, he has also given us enough in common to enable us to get along with one another. So you may have a friend who does something that you cannot do and you may be able to do something that s/he can't do, but there will also be plenty that you will be able to share together. So let's be grateful for all the things that make us unique and special and let's also celebrate our differences, which make life so interesting for us all.

CLOSING PRAYER OUTLINE
God, our Father, you have made us what we are and we thank you for all the skills and talents that you have given to each person here. Help us to learn what we can share with those around us, that together we may enjoy learning from one another. Amen.

32.
We Were All Like That Once!

CONTEXT

Any time of year, but it can be used very effectively to focus on the themes of tolerance, impatience and understanding. It works well with a small group of around 8–12 children during a morning service, but it can also be adapted for use in front of a larger school group.

YOU WILL NEED

A number of jigsaws (either three or five, ideally) in ascending order of difficulty, including one of extreme complexity.

Ask the children if they have done a jigsaw recently and ask those who respond what the jigsaw turned out to be when they put it together. Aren't jigsaws fun?

Then produce a very simple jigsaw with about four pieces in it, suitable for a very young child. You may like to ask for a volunteer to put it together. Draw the attention of the group to how straightforward it was. Then move on to another more difficult one and see if there is anyone who is willing to complete it.

Keep going until you reach the very last jigsaw, which should be beyond the reach of the average primary school child, i.e. one with 3,000 pieces. Ask them if there is anyone who has ever tried to do one of these really difficult jigsaws. There may well be, but it is unlikely that there will be a stampede of volunteers eager to tackle this enormous challenge!

Underline the fact that at every stage in our lives we learn through doing things that are suitable to the age and level we are at that time. There is no point in giving the very complicated puzzle to a child of eighteen months because he or she won't know what to do with it, except perhaps try to eat it! Neither would there be any point in giving a four-piece jigsaw to a 12 year old! In school the work we do is designed to suit us at whatever stage we're at. As we grow, the level of difficulty gradually increases as our brains work out how to do more complicated tasks.

Impress upon the children that they were all just starting school themselves once and that it is important to understand what difficulties other people may have. Encourage them to be patient with those who need a little more time to understand what is going on and remind them that they were once at that same stage themselves, so they should know what it feels like.

CLOSING PRAYER OUTLINE
God our Father, we thank you for the wonder of learning. Help us to be patient and understanding with those who learn at a different pace from us and to encourage those around us day by day. In the name of Jesus, we pray, Amen.

33.
What About a Game of Scrabble?

CONTEXT
Any time of year.

YOU WILL NEED
A bag of Scrabble letters, a flip chart and a marker.

Ask the children if any of them has ever played a game of Scrabble. Can they say which of the letters is the most valuable? Shake up the bag of Scrabble letters and ask for a volunteer to come up and take seven letters out of the bag. Write the seven letters up on the flip chart for everyone to see and then try and make as many words as you can out of them. Depending on what comes out of the bag, you might like to ask a range of children from different class groups to contribute suggestions.

Once you have a reasonable selection of words, you can move on to say that every time you pick letters out of the Scrabble bag, they come out in different combinations. You can't say ahead of time what you're going to get. The same goes for every new day. We start the day not quite knowing what we are going to be dealing with but we can usually make something out of what we've got. Some days will be harder than others.

There may be big things and difficult things that we have to deal with, but other times, we'll have things to look forward to and special treats to enjoy.

It is up to us to try and make something of every day that we've been given. Every new day is a gift, to be enjoyed and to be treasured. This is the day that the Lord has made! Let us rejoice and be glad in it!

CLOSING PRAYER OUTLINE

O God our Father, you have equipped each person with gifts and graces to share and to enjoy. Help us to meet each new morning with thankfulness and to live each day to the full. In the name of Jesus, we pray, Amen.

34.
Designer Labels

CONTEXT
Any time of year.

YOU WILL NEED
A selection of badges, e.g. denoting membership, achievement, support for charities, etc. Also a number of cards on which you have clearly written the various fruits of the spirit as mentioned in Galatians 5:22-23, a roll of adhesive tape and scissors.

Ask the children if they support a sports team and do a quick survey with a show of hands. Continue to say that very often, as supporters of a certain team we wear something which tells people which side we're on. What items do the children wear that makes their allegiance to a particular team clear?

Say that sometimes people wear badges, and show the children the badges that you have brought with you, representing a range of things that you support. Examples might be a charity pin or a scout badge. Explain that when we see people wearing special badges like these, we can tell a lot about them. The badge is pinned to their jumper or their sweatshirt and we can see at a glance what is important to them.

Continue on by saying that while such outward symbols mean we can tell what they're interested in, we can't tell what people are like inside. Ask them to imagine what it would be like if they wore their feelings like badges! Ask for a volunteer to come up to the front and tape the fruits of the Spirit all over his/her front. Ask one of the older children to read them aloud for the younger ones and explain where these words have come from. When we wear a badge, it is easy for people to know what interests us, but we Christians are also called to show people what we are like by the way we behave towards them.

So while we don't go around wearing badges like these ones here, it should still be clear to others by how we behave and by how we treat them that we are supporters of Jesus and that we are trying to live our lives in a way that pleases Him.

CLOSING PRAYER OUTLINE
Loving God, you have called us to follow you. Help us to show our love for you in everything we think, say and do, so that others will know by our example that we are your disciples. In the name of Jesus, Amen.

35.
Cracking the Code

CONTEXT
Any time of year.

YOU WILL NEED
Some card on which you will have about seven enlarged pictures of well-known signs and symbols e.g. a road sign, a car logo, a symbol from a box of washing powder, etc. You will also need a second set of symbols: a large picture of a fish, a scallop shell and a cross.

Describe one of the signs/logos you have brought with you to the children before showing it them. Ask them if they can work out what you are describing. When they have guessed correctly, go on to say that we live in a world where there are signs all around us.

Go on to describe signs as a kind of shortcut to help people identify and understand straight away. Even if you travel to a country where you don't speak the language, you should still be able to work out what it is that a sign is trying to tell you or recognise a familiar logo.

Show them the second set of symbols. Ask them if they can say what these symbols represent and supplement any suggestions with additional information. Explain that they would have been used by the early Christians as a kind of secret code.

Ask the children for suggestions as to why this might be. Build on what they suggest to explain that in the days of the early Church, anyone who followed Jesus could get into serious trouble. There could be spies anywhere who would have them arrested and put in prison, so they had to be very careful. So the early Christians developed a whole new language of signs and symbols that only they knew the meaning of. That meant that they could meet in secret with other people who were also trying to follow Jesus.

We all love cracking codes and trying to communicate with one another in secret languages. It can be a lot of fun. What, though, if our lives depended on it? For the early Christians, it was incredibly dangerous, but it is thanks to their bravery that the message of Jesus was able to spread from Palestine right around the world.

Finish by showing the children the cross, which is perhaps one of the most easily recognised signs of all.

CLOSING PRAYER OUTLINE
Loving Father, we thank you for those who risked their lives to follow you. Help us to be brave so that we can help others to understand the message of love and hope that your Son came to bring us. In his name we pray, Amen.

36.
The Jesus Nut

CONTEXT
Any time of year.

YOU WILL NEED
A nut (as in bolt) and a toy helicopter (optional).

Ask the children what they know about helicopters. What kinds of people use them? Have they got a toy one at home? Do they know anyone who can fly one? Have they ever been on a helicopter ride? Ask them to describe their experiences and their feelings as they go.

Then draw their attention to the blades of a helicopter. How many are there? What kind of a sound do they make? Ask the children to think about how important those blades are for the helicopter to work properly and stress the fact that if anything happened to interfere with them there could be serious trouble, so it's very important for those blades to be securely attached to the main part of the helicopter at all times.

Then take out the nut and explain that a nut, very similar to this one, but a little bit bigger, is what keeps the helicopter blades attached to the helicopter. It is absolutely vital for this nut to be in the right place and secure for the blades to stay on. If this is not in place, then the blades will become loose.

Pilots and mechanics have a special name for this nut. Ask the children for suggestions as to what a good name might be and explore with them the reasons why they have suggested those particular names. Finally tell them, if they haven't already suggested it, that this little nut is called the Jesus nut. It is called that because it is essential to the operation of the helicopter, just like Jesus is the essential component that we need in order for our lives to work.

We are a bit like machines in one sense: we are a collection of different parts which all come together to do different jobs, like seeing, walking, eating, holding and hearing. But people are different from machines because we have hearts and minds that enable us to make decisions about how we are to live our lives. Jesus came to teach us how to do that and if we have Jesus keeping our lives together, we will never fall apart.

CLOSING PRAYER OUTLINE
O loving God, you sent your only Son into our world to enter our lives and to show us how to try and make the world a better place. Help us to realise how important Jesus is in all our lives and to learn more about how to have him at the centre of all we do. In his name we pray, Amen.

37.

Standing On Our Own Two Feet

CONTEXT
Any time of year.

YOU WILL NEED
A puppet – preferably a string puppet, but hand puppets work better if you are considering involving the children.

Ask the children if they have ever seen a puppet show and ask one or two to share their experiences.

Introduce your new friend to the children and make him do a few things, like waving, clapping and bowing. If you have two puppets, you could ask an older child to come up and the two of you might attempt a dance routine!

Once the excitement has died down, you might move on to look at why the puppet can do the things he does. What enables him to wave or to dance? A skilful puppeteer can get a puppet to do all kinds of things. In the right hands, a puppet can be made to do almost anything.

Move on to say that, sometimes, people can be very like puppets. They do exactly whatever they are told to do. Of course, that is not always a bad thing. There are times when we all have to do what we're told. Ask the children for examples of those times when they must be obedient (these may include instructions from a teacher, lollipop lady, doctor, parent etc.). Explore with the children how that makes them feel.

But there are other times when we can be made to feel uncomfortable by instructions we are not happy to carry out. Ask the children for examples of times when they are told to do something that they know is wrong (these may include cheating in a test, telling a lie, stealing something) and once again, ask them how that makes them feel.

Explain to the children that as they grow up they will need to learn to be able to tell the difference between those things that they should do and those things that they should avoid doing. Unlike a puppet, they will need to be able to stand on their own two feet and to be able to make good decisions about all kinds of things throughout their lives. Reassure them that it is in a place like school that this journey begins, where they will have the guidance of their teachers and the support of their friends to help them make the right choices.

CLOSING PRAYER OUTLINE
Father God, as we grow and learn more about our world, give us courage to do what we feel to be right and help us to make the right choices in our lives. In the name of Jesus, Amen.

38.
That's Not Fair!

CONTEXT

Any time of year when you would like to focus on issues of justice and equality.

YOU WILL NEED

An eight-section bar of chocolate and an enlarged picture of the Fair Trade logo.

Note that this talk can have two possible endings, depending on the lesson you wish to emphasise. With older children, if you want to stress the aspect of injustice you can use the talk as it appears here. With younger children, however, you might find it easier to focus on the aspect of sharing, in which case it would be a good idea to have with you a box of chocolates to distribute at the end of the talk. Do be sure to have one for everybody in the audience!

Say that today you'd like to talk about sharing. Take out the bar of chocolate, unwrap it and talk about how delicious chocolate is as you are going along. Say that we are so used to seeing chocolate in our shops that we rarely pause to think about how it got there.

Well, let's think about that for a moment. Let's think in particular of the farmer who grows the cocoa beans that go into making the chocolate in the first place. You would think that he would be earning a pile of money, when you consider the millions of bars that are sold every day around the world. What a great job, you may think. Lots of people buying lots of chocolate must mean a lot of money for the farmer.

Explain to the children that there are many people involved in getting the chocolate bar into our shops and that every one of them gets a bit of money for what they do. Ask the children to imagine that each of the squares is worth about 20c and show them how little the farmer actually receives as follows:

- The shopkeeper where you buy your chocolate needs to make some money [eat square 1]
- So does the driver of the van who drove it to the shop [eat square 2]
- And what about the manager of the factory where the chocolate is made? [eat square 3]
- Then there are the people at the docks who loaded the cocoa beans on to the truck to get them to the factory [eat square 4]
- And the man who drove the truck from the cocoa farm to the ferry port [eat square 5]
- There is the manager of the truck hire company [eat square 6]
- And the manager of the cocoa bean farm where the beans were grown [eat square 7]
- And the farmer, the very person who grew and gathered the beans in the first place, ends up with a tiny part of the money that you have spent on your chocolate bar in the shop down the road [leave the last square uneaten for everyone to see].

Now that's not fair! So someone a number of years ago decided to try and do something about the situation and to encourage us all to buy food labelled with a special logo. When we see this logo anywhere on food it tells us that under new rules the farmer and others further down the line must get a fair wage for the work they do. This is called Fair Trade. As Christians, we are called to fight unfairness wherever we find it. We can do our bit by buying things (and not just food) that ensure that the money made is more evenly shared out and by passing the message of Fair Trade on to others.

CLOSING PRAYER OUTLINE

Help us, Father, to remember with thankfulness those who work so hard to provide us with our food and give us a real passion for justice and fairness in our world. Amen.

39.
Seven Spools of Thread

CONTEXT
This is a tale from Ghana associated with the African-American celebration of Kwanzaa, which takes place over a week after Christmas. Although it can be used at any time of the year to illustrate the themes of unity, teamwork or problem solving.

YOU WILL NEED
Seven spools of thread of the following colours: black, white, red, orange, yellow, blue and green. It is also effective to weave strips of paper in the same seven colours together in advance of the assembly to show the children at the end.

In a small village in the heart of Ghana, there lived a man who had seven sons. The man's wife died, leaving him on his own with the boys who were always squabbling. The boys argued and fought from sunrise until sunset and this was a source of great disappointment to their father.

One sad day, the old man died and at sunrise the next morning the village chief called the brothers before him. 'Your father has left you an inheritance,' he told them. Immediately the boys began to argue over who should be left the most in their father's will. Soon all seven were rolling around on the ground, hitting and kicking each other.

'Stop it!' shouted the chief and the sons stopped to listen. 'Your father has decreed that all his property and possessions will be divided amongst you equally. But first, by moonrise tonight, you must learn how to make gold out of these spools of silk thread. If you fail, you will be turned out of your home as beggars. Starting with the eldest, he handed out one spool to each son: blue, red, yellow, orange, green, black and white. 'From now on, you must not argue among yourselves, because if you do, everything your father owns will be given to the poor of the village instead and you will get nothing. So go! You have very little time!'

When the seven sons arrived home, something unusual happened. They sat together without saying unkind words to one another. After a while, the oldest son said, 'Let us shake hands and make peace,' and they did. After that they began to try and work out together what it was they could do to fulfil their father's wishes. Gradually, through careful listening and compromise they hit upon a solution: they could build a loom and weave the seven spools of thread into colourful fabric, which they could then sell for gold.

They took turns weaving the cloth and beautiful patterns began to emerge. Soon the brothers had several pieces of beautiful multi-coloured cloth, which they packed up and took to the local market just as the sun was beginning to set. The cloth caused a sensation, so much so that the King's treasurer bought it all … for a bag of gold.

The brothers ran home as the moon began to rise in the sky and arrived back at the feet of the chief. 'You have learnt your lesson well,' he said. 'But what about the poor?' asked the youngest son. 'We shall teach them to turn thread into gold,' said the eldest. This they did and the village became famous for its beautiful multi-coloured cloth, which has come to be known throughout the world as Kente.

CLOSING PRAYER OUTLINE

Loving Father, help us to appreciate the gifts you have given to each one of us and to understand what we can all achieve by working together. Open our minds and our hearts to the lessons you need us to learn this day. Amen.

40.
Lessons From a Mouse

CONTEXT
Any time of year.

YOU WILL NEED
The story below, based on the well-known children's tale *The Enormous Turnip.*

This very simple assembly uses the traditional story of *The Enormous Turnip* as its base, although there are many other storybooks that can be used to equal effect. *The Enormous Turnip* is particularly useful, however, as it illustrates two very important themes which need to be reinforced in a context such as a school: the way in which the success of the job to be done can often depend on the contribution and efforts of the smallest member of the group AND the value of teamwork. Using a well-known story makes the message particularly accessible for the youngest children while also providing an instructive illustration for the older children who are listening.

The story revolves around a farmer who plants some turnips, of which one in particular grows to monstrous proportions. When it comes to harvest time, he solicits the assistance of his wife to pull it up. When that proves ineffective, he asks a local child to lend his weight to the task. When this doesn't work either, the farmer involves a smaller child, then a dog, a cat and finally, a mouse. It is the mouse's input that turns out to be crucial: after a collective last effort on the part of everyone involved, there is a satisfying wrenching sound and the turnip, finally, pops out.

Encourage the children to contribute as you go by asking them if they think the turnip will budge as each character joins in. At the very end, ask them what we might learn from the story. Their insights can often be a surprise!

CLOSING PRAYER OUTLINE
Our loving Father, you have placed us in families and amongst other people so that we can learn from one another and enjoy working together. Help us to remember that everyone has something to contribute and to be an encouragement to those around us. Amen.

41.
The Things Mothers Do!

CONTEXT
Any time of year when you want to focus on mothers. This assembly can also be adapted for a whole number of other uses.

YOU WILL NEED
Seven A4 sheets on which you have written the letters that make up the word MOTHERS for everyone to see.

For this very simple talk, you might consider involving seven volunteers from amongst the children to hold up a letter each. Hand them out in random order so that it is not immediately clear what they spell. Ask for suggestions to get them in the correct order.

Once they have spelt out the word correctly, ask the children for suggestions as to some of the things that mothers do for them which begin with each letter. Suggestions may include:

M	making meals
O	operating a taxi service
T	tidying
H	helping with homework
E	encouraging
R	reassuring
S	shopping

Spend some time thinking about this, acknowledging the importance of mothers in all our lives.

CLOSING PRAYER OUTLINE

God our Father, we thank you for our mothers and for all those people in our lives who mother us in different ways. Help us to appreciate them all and to do our best to show them that we care for them by doing little acts of kindness day by day. In the name of Jesus, who taught us to love one another, Amen.

42.
I'm Not Feeling Great Today

CONTEXT
Any time of the year.

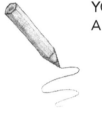

YOU WILL NEED
A first aid kit.

Start off by saying that you nearly didn't come into school today at all because you were feeling so rotten. Elaborate on some of your symptoms (e.g. sore throat, tickly cough, streaming nose, aching joints). Rummage around in the first aid kit and try to find something you can take to alleviate your symptoms. Pick out some items that are clearly unsuitable (like tweezers, insect repellent and Elastoplast) and then pick out a packet of Lemsip or Beechams Powders and sound relieved that you have found something that will hopefully do you some good.

Expand on the idea of illness and on how the whole body can suffer when even just one small part (like the nose) is affected. Ask the children to remember times when they may have had a splinter in a finger, a bad bee sting or a toothache. Sometimes we can be in such pain that it can be hard to think of anything else. Sometimes even the tiniest injury can affect our whole body.

Explain that the same goes for a place like a school. A school is a body of people who are all affected by what happens to any one there. If someone has a serious accident, the whole school knows about it. If someone's mum has a new baby, everyone is delighted! If someone in the class is upset, that upset can spread to the other members of the class and everyone can sense that something is not quite right.

Tell the children that, as a result, we need to be careful of the little things we do and say to one another. We don't want to add to anyone's hurt or sadness – we want to help them and encourage them instead.

CLOSING PRAYER OUTLINE
Our loving Father, help us to understand that what we say and do matters very much. Make us thoughtful and considerate to the feelings of others, make us careful in the little things of life, and to do what we can to make this world a better and a happier place for us all. In Jesus' name, we pray, Amen.

43.
Taste and See!

CONTEXT
Any time of the year.

YOU WILL NEED
An electric blender, some juice, some plastic cups and an assortment of chopped fruit to make a smoothie (including a lot of banana).

Start by asking everyone if they like smoothies and say that because you know that they're so healthy for us, you're going to start your day by making one right here and now.

Put in all the fruit into the blender, together with a little fruit juice to make it thinner, and blend it all up in front of the children. Then pour some into a few glasses and share it out amongst one or two others to taste. Ideally use children from different class groups and maybe even a teacher.

Have a little conversation about what fruits they think might have gone into the smoothie. The taste of the banana should be sufficiently strong for them to be able to identify it as the predominant flavour. Talk about how quickly they were able to identify the taste of the banana.

Expand on the idea of taste by moving on to explore other kinds of food that can change the flavours of what we eat. Ask the children for examples of other strong flavours. Then move on to consider salt and how it can change the taste of our food.

People are a bit like salt. Jesus called his followers the 'salt of the earth'. What do you think he meant? Well, he meant that the people who followed him should be people who would add flavour to the world. He wanted people to be able to look at his followers and say 'Yes, that's it!' He wanted his people to be so distinctive in the ways that they behaved day by day that everyone would know immediately that those people must be in some way connected to him.

Just like the banana in the smoothie, we are called to add a special flavour to the world and to do what we can to point people to Jesus.

CLOSING PRAYER OUTLINE
Loving Father, help us to live our lives so that other people can see that we are trying to follow your example. We pray, in the name of Jesus, who called us 'the salt of the earth'. Amen.

44.
The Hunter

CONTEXT
Any time of year and ideal when dealing with the issues of understanding, sympathy and shared experience.

YOU WILL NEED
The story below.

This story takes place in the African countryside and starts early one morning, when a little girl called Jamina goes with her grandfather to collect honey.

'Will I see elephants?' Jamina asked her grandfather.

'You'll be lucky if you do,' her grandfather replied. 'With all the hunters around, there aren't many to be seen these days.'

'Hunters!' cried Jamina excitedly, 'I want to be a hunter when I grow up.' Then she began to imagine that she had her own gun. Hiding behind the bushes, she imagined aiming at a mighty elephant, tracking a huge rhino and stalking a pride of lions. When she turned back to look for her grandfather, he was nowhere to be seen. She had wandered too far into the forest and there was no sign of him or of the honey birds they had come to find. In fact, there was nothing at all but silence.

Then Jamina heard a sound, a sad and desperate cry coming from not too far away. She held her breath and listened. Her parents had always warned her not to go alone into the bush but the sound was so mournful and desperate that Jamina couldn't resist finding out what was making it. She walked in the direction of the sound until she came to a clearing, where she saw a tiny elephant trying to wake his mother who lay still on the ground. The hunters had been there and, like Jamina, this little elephant was lost and afraid. Jamina realised that the calf would not survive on his own so she decided that she would try to lead him home and perhaps they might find his family on the way.

Very shakily, the baby elephant got to his feet and with Jamina's encouragement they began their journey. Then the rain came and the ground became slippery underfoot, but still they carried on. Sometimes she would hear a sound and think that it might be a herd of elephants, but it was only the wind in the long grass. After a day or two, they did come across a herd of zebra and all through that afternoon Jamina and the baby elephant travelled alongside it.

That evening they were resting after a long day's walk when Jamina heard the sound of voices. 'My parents!' she thought excitedly. But the dark shadows in the distance were not her parents, but poachers, on the lookout for elephants to kill. Even the baby elephant seemed to sense that something was not right and they both remained absolutely silent and still until the poachers had moved away. Exhausted, hungry and frightened they spent that night huddled close together and fell in and out of a restless sleep.

Very early the next morning, Jamina was awoken by a gentle but persistent rumble, and in the half light she could see some dark shapes swaying from side to side. She discovered that during the night a troupe of elephants had come that way and that the little elephant calf beside her was struggling to his feet to join them. 'Take this little one with you,' murmured Jamina softly as the elephants made to move on, 'and keep him safe.'

By the first light of dawn, Jamina's mother found her sleeping in the grass. 'I was playing hunters and I got lost,' she said, and she stayed very close to her mother all the way home. 'I don't want to be a hunter anymore,' she said softly to herself as they reached the village.

CLOSING PRAYER OUTLINE

Loving Father, this story reminds us of what it is like to be lost, lonely and afraid. Help us, we pray, to understand better the feelings of those around us, that we may grow to see things through their eyes and learn how best to help. Amen.

45.
Leaving Our Mark

CONTEXT
This very simple children's talk can be used at any time of the year, but could be used to particularly good effect in the run-up to the summer holidays when the children's thoughts are turning to the outdoors and to the seaside.

YOU WILL NEED
A selection of footwear of different sizes each of which should have a different kind of sole. Alternatively, ask the children to show you the soles of their shoes and you can use their shoes instead!

Ask the children to have a look at their shoes. Ask those who are wearing runners to put up their hands. Does anyone have shoes on which are fastened with velcro? How about slip-on shoes? Multi-coloured shoes? Boots? Draw the children's attention to the fact that for most people what is important to them is the top of their shoes. The bit with the style, colour and shape. However, what you'd like to focus on today is the bit they rarely see – the sole. Show them some of the soles on the shoes and footwear.

Ask the children to imagine that they are on a beach. Isn't it interesting how much you can tell from other people's footprints?

You can tell immediately if the person is an adult by the size of the shoe and by how deep the footprint goes. You can tell if someone is out walking the dog because you'll have human and animal footprints together, or if someone has taken a small child for a walk. We can tell a lot about the people who have gone before us by the marks they leave behind.

Continue to say that people leave lots of other things behind them as they go through life. Ask the children to explore what other kinds of trails or legacies people can leave. Suggestions might include: teaching people a skill which they can then use themselves; setting up a hospital which people can use for years afterwards; writing a book that will be around for a very long time.

Encourage the children to see themselves as trail makers and tell them that as they grow up and move onwards through their lives, they too will leave a trail behind them for others to follow. Hopefully, it will be a trail of good things that will help and encourage others as they too journey through life.

CLOSING PRAYER OUTLINE

Loving Father, we thank you for all those people who are important in our lives and who have made us what we are. Help us, in our turn, to be a good example to others. In the name of Jesus, Amen.

46.
All Together Now!

CONTEXT
Any time of year and ideally with a small group, perhaps in the context of a morning service.

YOU WILL NEED
An apron, a bag containing everything you need to bake a cake, and a cake already made (in a tin placed out of sight) for the children to share at the end. Cake decorations and flavourings always add extra interest!

This talk is very easy and appeals to a wide range of ages. Start by asking the children if they have ever made a cake. As you put on the apron, ask them what a cook needs in order to make a cake. As they call out the ingredients, take them out of the bag and put them on a table or shelf for everyone to see.

Having mentioned the basics, you might like to move on to ask the children if there is anything extra that they might use when baking a cake. Suggestions may include icing sugar, lemon flavouring, candles and decorations. If you have those in the bag, produce them and add them to the other ingredients.

Now ask the children to imagine a cake with no sugar in it. What would that taste like?

Has anyone ever tasted a cake with too much flavouring in it? Ask them how the cake might look if the baking powder was left out. Can anyone describe what happens when a cake is put into the oven at the wrong temperature?

Explain that in order to bake a really fluffy and tasty cake, a lot of very important things need to happen. The right ingredients must be put into the cake and measured correctly, and care must be taken to make sure that when you've made your mixture, the oven is at the right temperature to produce the right result.

In this way, life is very much like making a cake: everyone is an important ingredient and has a part to play in how successful things turn out to be. So let's remember the importance of every single person here and the contribution that each one of us can make. When we all mix together we can produce something really special.

CLOSING PRAYER OUTLINE
Loving Father, thank you for our school/church/group and for our special place within it. Help us to work to do wonderful things together, in Jesus's name, Amen.

Now, who'd like some cake?

47.

The Little Bushrat

CONTEXT

CONTEXT
Any time of year when you need to focus on 'the little guy' who saves the day. It is based on a story set in the Australian outback, but there are lots of other stories from closer to home that are equally effective.

YOU WILL NEED
The story below (or one with a similar message).

Ask the children if anyone has ever been to the very middle of Australia. Tell them that is one of the driest places on the planet – the soil is dusty and reddish and life is very harsh for any animals that manage to survive there. Yet some animals do live there and one of those is the little brown bushrat. Has anyone here got a pet gerbil? A bushrat is a bit like a gerbil, so you get the idea of its size – the bushrat is a small animal.

Our story begins with our little bushrat making his way home across the Australian outback on a hot and dusty afternoon. While he was walking along he came to a small cluster of eucalyptus trees. Under these trees, where there was a nice shaded spot out of the sun, a number of other animals had gathered and were deep in conversation. As the little bushrat got closer, he realised that they were busily discussing what it was that each of them did best. So he sat down and listened.

'I can jump higher than anyone else,' announced the kangaroo, bounding over a nearby bush. 'Well, I'm by far the fastest runner,' declared the emu, who raced around the trees at top speed. 'I can hang upside down by my tail,' said the possum giving a little demonstration. 'In terms of beauty, no one even comes close to me,' declared the lyrebird, raising his magnificent tail feathers in a stunning display. And so it continued. The rainbow lorikeet was the most colourful, the kookaburra had the loudest laugh, the echidna had the longest nose and the koala ... well, the koala could sleep for longer than anyone else.

The little bushrat wiped away a tear. 'I'm not any good at anything,' he sighed, feeling sad as he continued his journey home. Suddenly he heard a commotion behind him and a flutter of feathers. He turned around to see the wompoo fruit dove come bursting into the clearing. 'FIRE!' she squawked.

At first everyone was completely still ... but then there was panic! The kangaroo jumped up and down, the emu ran round and round in circles, the kookaburra laughed nervously, the lyrebird flapped his tail feathers in and out and the koala, despite all the excitement, fell asleep.

The bushrat, however, lifted his little nose into the air to sniff and worked out that the fire was in a clearing where the blazing sun had set fire to a pile of dry leaves. It wasn't a big fire, but as every animal in the Australian outback knows, the smallest fire can very quickly turn into a bushfire if it's not put out.

Through the clump of eucalyptus trees the little bushrat spied a silvery light and realising that there was a stream nearby, he leapt into action. He started digging and digging and digging. And just when he thought he couldn't dig any more, there was a sudden whoosh. The water from the stream gushed into the clearing and the fire was out in seconds.

One by one the animals returned and saw the tired and soggy bushrat standing by the smoking twigs. It was the possum that spoke first: 'Bushrat saved us! He's the bravest one of us all.' There was a huge cheer and the little bushrat glowed with pride. And that evening, as the sun went down over the outback, the little bushrat smiled to himself, 'I *am* the best at something after all,' he thought, 'I just didn't know it.'

CLOSING PRAYER OUTLINE
Our loving Father, you have made each one of us special in our own way. Help us to appreciate the gifts that you have given to us and to others, and to use those wonderful gifts to bring pleasure and encouragement to our families and friends. Amen.

48.
You Win Some, You Lose Some!

CONTEXT
Any time of year, but it could be used to particularly good effect at a time when you might want to focus on sport, sportsmanship, winning and losing

YOU WILL NEED
Some item of sports equipment, such as a rugby ball, football or hockey stick. What you use may depend on the precise circumstances of the time and/or the relevance to the children involved. You may also like to use a flipchart to record the children's responses.

Do a quick survey about the kind of sports that the children enjoy and, if appropriate, ask for a show of hands by those who are involved in the school's sports teams. Ask these children what they feel to be the benefits of playing sports. Responses may include getting fresh air and exercise, teamwork, being able to excel at something and so on.

Move on to ask what the advantages of winning at sports are? Encourage a range of responses. Follow this up by asking the children whether there is anything good about being on the losing side in a match and see how they respond.

Now ask them if they learn more by being on the winning team or by being on the losing side. It is important to underline the fact that it can be by losing or doing something wrong that we discover how to do things right. We all make mistakes but we can learn a lot from these and use what we have learnt to try and do better next time.

Conclude by congratulating those who have won or by encouraging those who have lost and say that it is in our wins and in our losses that we grow and develop into fully rounded and balanced people.

CLOSING PRAYER OUTLINE

Thank you, God our Father, for games to play and leisure time to enjoy. Help us to understand the lessons we can learn from both winning and losing, that we may grow up to be the adults you would like us to be. Amen.

49.
Ouch! That Hurt!

CONTEXT
Any time of the year when you feel the need to focus on the way people treat each other.

YOU WILL NEED
No equipment necessary.

Begin by giving the children a big wave. Hopefully they will wave back! Use that opening to draw their attention to all the ways in which we use our hands on a daily basis. As the children gathered, you might have noticed a girl plaiting someone else's hair or a boy tying his shoelaces, for example.

Ask for other examples of things people do with their hands in school. Suggestions may include writing, throwing and catching a ball, painting, eating food, operating the water fountain and sharpening a pencil. Stress the fact that we are so used to having our hands doing so much work for us that we often forget all about them.

Hands can also be used for other things, too. Ask the children if they can think of any activity involving their hands that might not be a good thing to do. Suggestions here may include poking, pinching, slapping, punching and stealing.

Remind the children that we are able to do good things and bad things with our hands; things that make other people happy (like wrapping a present or writing a card) but also things that can hurt people and make them miserable (like punching or taking something that is special to somebody away from them).

Encourage the children to think a little more carefully about the things that they do when there are other people about. Stress that if everyone took just a little more care, there would be a lot less hurt and a lot more fun.

End the assembly by asking everyone to join you in a thunderous round of applause!

CLOSING PRAYER OUTLINE
Our loving Father, your Son Jesus went about bringing healing and blessing to others. Help us to think more carefully about the things we do so that we may bring pleasure and encouragement to others too. Amen.

50.
No One Else Has One of Those!

CONTEXT
Any time of year.

YOU WILL NEED
A sheet of paper or thick card on which you have drawn a very simple impression of a fingerprint. You might like to do a little survey amongst the children to see what common links they share. This could be reinforced by the use of a clipboard and pen or a flipchart, depending on time and resources.

Ask the children a number of general questions about themselves and their interests. Some of the questions might include the following:

- How many of you came to school on foot today?
- Does anyone here have a hamster at home?
- Who ate cornflakes for breakfast this morning?
- Have any of you ever been on a car ferry?
- How many of you can swim?
- Does anyone here play the guitar?

Point out that most people have something in common with at least one other person. Very often we are friends with people who share the same interests as we do. Sharing hobbies and spending time with people who see things in a similar way to us is a good thing and it can also be a lot of fun.

Then move on to say that there is one thing that is unique to us, which no one else has. Can anyone guess what that might be? Some of the older children may be able to work it out but if the group needs prompting you can display the image of the fingerprint.

Stress that our fingerprints are unique to us. When we think about all the people in the world, each one with a different set of fingerprints, that really is amazing! Use this to reinforce the special nature of each individual person in the world and how important each one of us is to God.

CLOSING PRAYER OUTLINE

O God, you have made each one of us unique. Help us to remember that everyone is equally precious to you. In the name of Jesus, we pray, Amen.

Index of Key Themes

The numbers refer to the numbered talks.

Index of Key Themes

Sources

Davidson, Susanna, *The Story of Hanukkah* (London: Usborne, 2007).

Geraghty, Paul, *The Hunter* (London: Red Fox, 1994).

Hodges, Margaret, *Silent Night* (Grand Rapids, MI: Eerdmans Books for Young Readers, 1997).

Horn, Sandra Ann, *Babushka* (Oxford: Barefoot Books, 2002).

Ripper, Georgie, *Little Brown Bushrat* (London: Macmillan Children's Books, 2002).

Shelf Medearis, Angela, *Seven Spools of Thread: A Kwanzaa Story* (Park Ridge, IL: Albert Whitman & Company, 2000).

Silf, Margaret, *One Hundred Wisdom Stories from Around the World* (Oxford: Lion, 2003).

Tews, Susan, *The Gingerbread Doll* (New York: Clarion Books, 1993).